Escape
Roots

poems by

Lois Young-Tulin

Fithian Press • Santa Barbara, California • 1994

Design and typography by Bill Spahr

Published by Fithian Press, a division of Daniel and Daniel Publishers, Inc.
Post Office Box 1525
Santa Barbara, California 93102

LIBRARY OF CONGRESS CATALOGING-IN-PUBLICATION DATA
    YOUNG-TULIN, LOIS
        Escape roots : poems / by Lois Young-Tulin.
            p.   cm.
        ISBN 1-56474-078-1
        1. Women, Jewish—United States—Poetry. I. Title
    PS3575.O867E83   1994
    811'.54—dc20   93-30663
                                                    CIP

ESCAPE ROOTS

Because of my branches, Karen Daniel and Billy;
and because of my roots, Marion and Milton Young
and Judith Young Mallin
and
because of JS, BW, Leslie, Peter, Gloria, Barak, the Women's
Group, the Tulin Sisters, the In-Laws Club
and my guru, Richard Longchamps.

THIS IS FOR DAVID

CONTENTS

Cocktails to Go

ROOTS

KIEV

I see my grandfather's face
eyes wrinkled in laughter
wide lips puffing a thick cigar
I see his face on the streets of Kiev
I walk among his brethren
sons of Cossacks who taunted him
daughters of gentiles who tempted him.
"See their belts," he says, "they are
hard leather like their hearts."
I pick up traces he left behind
I hear his name whispered on street corners
I feel his hardened hands on my shoulders
he leads me into a farmers' market to a family
with clear eyes as his were and soft round cheeks
I hear his lilting voice, taste his practical
jokes that fed his hungry children.

He died poor and full of laughter
too young to lose his life
too old to change his job
I see him in a small room
in Norwich, Connecticut
cutting black bread, offering
me some. He's wearing short white
shirtsleeves, gray pants held up
by soft red suspenders.

NEWS CAFE, MIAMI BEACH

The coffee is served in a glass mug.
A pentimento effect surfaces, forcing
a long hyperbolic arc across my
memories. Such laconic split-
seconds of perception serve as a segue
into images of Kristallnacht.

I sift through a dark lexicon of possible deeds
in search of a more palpable fixation;
galactic reverberations tilt precariously
and ricochet off a mirrored image of my aged
grandfather, sugar cube held in his mouth as
he sipped hot tea from a tall crystal
tumbler before glass and crystal shattered
in the street outside the Jewish shops that
resonating night when sequined messages
of hatred glared through the haze of psalmic wisdom.

The glassy-eyed merchants' sabotaged
assimilation broke the symbiosis
between culture and counterculture,
between ethnicity and ethics.

It is half a century later, and sounds
of breaking glass cause countervailing
slippages into a state of vertigo. A
warning from the blue sky excoriates
me to be neither smugly complacent
nor perfunctorily off guard.

I call upon my own self-canceling narcissism,
an oxymoron that helped me make it
through my 30s and 40s,
witnessed the semitic
hatred that renews itself like snakeskin
and threatens to disrupt my
mortal transience by bringing
on a bout of agoraphobia.

IN THE SYNAGOGUE

On Kol Nidre I am one of two women
called to the Bimah to hold the Torah.
The fire of tradition burns my hands as
I hold the holy book in my arms.
The scrolls personified as royalty
wear a silver crown, a velvet mantle.
I look upward to the small balcony,
see back in time, behold the women
in segregated seats.

> A *street urchin wanders into shul,*
> his hot liquorbreath gasps.
> He crosses himself and holds his
> soiled baseball cap to his chest.

I return the following day for the memorial
service for the dead. I mouth the Yizkor prayer
for my father who appears in a mist, his eyes
burning with fever, his hands warm with love.

I remember, I whisper. I have cherished your
soul for eleven years, and I remember.
He guides my fist to my heart as I recite
the Yom Kippur prayer of repentance,

> *"Forgive me, Father*
> *Ah-vee-nu-mahl-kenu."*

ESCAPE FROM SOBIBOR

Sixteen SS men at the Nazi death camp.
    125 Ukrainian mercenaries do the guarding.
    Kapos are foremen over work parties.

You are not allowed to cry.
    Trains unload. Fatal selections are made daily.
    Sobibor is lethal for 250,000 inmates.

        There are no babies in Sobibor.

Prisoners do everything running. 25 lashes.
    If you cannot run, you are shot. Everyday
    is an agony of conscience.

Camp No. 3, northern compound used to gas
    with carbon monoxide and bodies
    burn in huge outdoor pit.

Sobibor is now planted over with pine trees
    which refuse to grow in its soil,
    soil encircled by trees
    that do not hide death.

        There were no babies in Sobibor.

YAD VASHEM

The Sea of Galilee receives
from Jordan's headwaters.
Unto them, the children
with the hollow eyes, will I
give a time and an age…
Rachel Rosenfeld…age four…Poland
Uziel Weil…age seven…Berlin
that they shall not be taken from us.

The Sea of Galilee gives
water to the Dead Sea.
Sara Burger…age sixteen…Warsaw
Samuel Steiner…age three…Vienna
that they shall be received
in our houses and within our walls,
not exiled by forgetful generations.

The Dead Sea receives
water from the Galilee.
They shall be redeemed from the Holocaust
by the secret of remembrance…
Miriam Goldsmith…age eleven…Hungary
Ben Metzger…age thirteen…Munich
a place and a name given to them
that they shall not be cut off.

The Dead Sea waters evaporate
in the mist.
Abraham Feldman…age nine…Amsterdam…

TIME OF INNOCENCE

My grandfather emigrated from Minsk.
He spoke the tongue of old people:
Yiddish. He remembered life in a
Russian village where cholera killed
those who drank the water, where
Cossacks mounted pogroms.

My grandfather was a slow moving,
slow talking man, partial to backless
house slippers. Photographs of the old
country show oddly dressed men and women
with hair hanging over their ears.

He spat on pictures of swastikas. He said,
"The brownshirt heathen, spit on them!"

When my cousin was born, a mohel came
to perform the circumcision. My
grandfather held the baby, placed a wine
soaked crust in the baby's mouth;
the old man's balding head,
the baby's downy pate, sunken chins.
The mohel helped himself to extra honeycake.
"Schnorer," said my grandfather, and he
turned, clapped his hands;
the celebration began.

SISTERCHILD

HONOR THY FATHER

I.

A daughter hears her father's confession.
He might have survived a double life.
He gambled his name for American convenience.
Sundays he wore the green plaid shirt which
brought angry moods. I shop for that shirt
when the full moon has too long been gone
to endless skies where his soul floats
if that is mortality.

II.

He reviewed his tired memories
in a New York City hospital,
our blood types compatible,
transfusions back and forth.
I, death helper, was alone
with Dostoevsky.
Nietzsche called
to release him.

III.

His fingers played with fogginess
around his eyes, attached
to a breathing machine.
He directed me with his eyes,
commanded me to pull the plug,
an order from father
to daughter.
He wanted to go home.

HONOR THY MOTHER

I.

I help her into the porcelain bathtub,
her body a miniature of the broad-hipped
woman I remember. She walks with
measured steps, this same woman beside
whom I walked in two-step to keep pace,
careful now lest she slip and break a bone.

She fades into her bedsheets,
a small woman, frightened
of the onset of disease.
Twice a day she checks her temperature
with the old thermometer still in its
black case I remember from childhood.

She is obsessed with cleaning out her papers,
stacks of receipts, bank statements,
fifteen years wrapped with rubber bands,
amassed since my father's death.

Her water-blue eyes seem larger now,
behind thick bifocals. She presses her
nose against each ledger page to decipher
the numbers. We pack discards into shopping
bags for the compactor. She worries that
someone will rifle through her life
and come to some conclusion.

She fears night, sleeps with lights on,
television a continuous glow. I fall asleep
to her labored breathing, awaken at dawn
to prepare a breakfast tray. I am nurturer,
grateful for a chance to shower her with focused
love, the kind that heals, the sort that speaks
in silence of the mother-daughter bond
tightly woven into a survival rope as
difficult to cut as an umbilical cord.

II.

Mother, I have come to care for you as you search
among dark shadows for demons. Feel my
hands rub your tired feet. I am struck by the sameness
of our bone structure. Taste the trust
we pass back and forth.
I have stored up all you have given me.
I play it back to you.

MENTAL HOSPITAL

a middle-aged woman stares
at institutional green walls
there are two pay telephones in a hallway
patients allotted 10 minutes   a woman stands
in paper slippers   shifts from
foot to foot   drops coins in slot
telephone rings on other end   everyone
she knows is out somewhere getting on
with life   she scratches at her face
hair disheveled

it is my sister who swallows capsules
who is numb with fear   who prays for death
to take her to a peaceful place to rid her
of demons   who shuffles down the hall
whose eyes try to focus on what went wrong
what spun around her anger 'til it plunged
deep into her depressed soul

it is my mother who comes with homemade egg salad
spread on thin rye   who visits insane asylums
who cannot weep   who brings trinkets
who brushes my sister's hair   she is 75
arthritic fingers   large breasts heavy with grief

it is voluntary commitment made by a woman
alone whose husband is gone   whose children
are lost   whose possessions are an albatross
it is my sister's duty to make up a metal bed
she is a woman who never made a bed
who hired others for such tasks

it is a family of females men dead
it comforts them to leave schedules
to authorities   meals to dining room
medication monitored visitations
it is my sister
it is our mother

A WOMAN DOES HER TIME

anger thrown in her face when she misbehaved
when she would not fall into a line
to be carefully walked.

    she ignored parental displeasure
    driven to reach her goal, she
    felt shame at who she was.

she married at seventeen, slept with a man
named Joe who was after money

    he beat her in the bedroom
    whipped her onto that line
    to be carefully walked
    she was a good girl.

she lives in an insane asylum
inmates are her friends
doctors and nurses are her parents

    she feels at home with
    the numbness of medication
    the dread of shock treatments
    arching her broken back

she is not ready to get better
until she has done her time.

AS A MOTHER

AS A MOTHER

Children of mine
he-child, she-child
accept that I
do not know solutions.
Bewildered, you look to me
for the moment;
yet I can merely help
you bide your time.

A TEST OF FAITH

Two birds
premature, voiceless
fallen from their nest
two dead already
two struggling
holding on to life
to each other.

I feel my husband's eyes on me
as if he fears I will let
him down, drop the birds
or worse be unable
to pull together
the courage to pick them up.

I hear God's voice
urging me on
depending on me to
be His hands
I put on gloves   remember
reading somewhere that once
touched by human hands
birds are rejected
by their mother.

I scoop them up
in unison as they
cling together.
I smell essence
of placenta, raw
birthing odors.
Their voiceless
throats throb
as they lift their
still-soft beaks
and mouth silent protest.

Returned to their nest
they root around
for nourishment
for assurance.

It is a spiritual
second chance
to even the score
for I owe a life.

EXPANSION

Spring awakens memories
dead in winter snow
echo of harvest time
waits up ahead despite
a nagging feeling that
the seeds did not take root.

I was a mother
one daughter
two sons circled
my legs
collie dog
shed hair
on season.

The seasons do not
wait to change
but come and go
despite it all
as if bored
with family matters.

I am a mother
one daughter grown
two sons away from home
collie dog
dead.

I cannot call back lost
seasons. I cannot redo
the weaning,
despite this drought.

SAN FRANCISCO TRIP IN '92

Three generations of women
My mother
My daughter
Me.
My daughter is four months away from
turning the age
my mother was
when I was
born.

WHEN THE CHILDREN ARE GROWN

When the children are grown,
I used to say, and the frost
is on the pumpkin, but there was no
time to prepare for a new harvest;
no time to plant new seeds for the garden;
and twisted vines need weeds removed
and dirt dug up around the beds.

I used to be able to see into the future,
when the children were grown,
the oldest she-child, working
in a foreign city, writing letters
on palimpsest. The first son
studying in a New England college
while the youngest he-child shoots
baskets on a midwestern court. I used
to think how far away it all was, how
endless the tasks of cooking, ironing, cleaning.

Now a young man comes home twice yearly;
another lives in a rented room in a
small college town. Their bedrooms are
untouched, awaiting vacations when they come
to celebrate adulthood. I am just
catching up with myself, unable any longer
to see into the future, having arrived
at the present, a future come too soon.

BUILDING BRIDGES

It is our last joint public venture
in Philadelphia—motherdaughter
daughtermother
ZipporahMiriamZipporah
MiriamZipporahMiriam.
In three weeks you move
across this continent, far
from my vision, yet close
to my heart-soul connection.
We smile at each other
across the sea of women's hands
as Bella Abzug speaks as a
woman Jew leader, as a daughtermother.
Global feminist women, we are
so many women; a majority in the work force;
victims of violence, poorer than men.
We do not seek special privileges
we demand rights as we marry
Judaism and feminism.
They name unborn fetus person
before women are named people.
We are called forth to change
the nature of power before power
changes our nature.
We have something to say
about peaceworldpeace,
peace in the family. We
maintain Shalom bayit.
Our eyes meet speak softly
and carry a lipstick.
daughtermotherdaughtermother
ZipporahMiriamZipporah
MiriamZipporahMiriam.

18

She took eighteen pills.
She took herself to the hospital.
I found her in the emergency ward,
clad in a white sheet.
She smiled.
Her father came,
as she hoped he would.
Her brothers sat
outside praying.
She cut me deep.
She violated us.
I birthed her from my womb.
She had no right to kill
my baby.
My uterus contracts nightly
in pains of almost losing her.
She took eighteen pills.
She took herself to the hospital.
She took herself from me,
as punishment for birthing her.
Our eyes meet by accident these days.
She is lost to me.
She took eighteen pills.
She is not yet eighteen.

JOURNEY INTO UNKNOWN WATERS

One ventured out
took sharp turns
carefully meted out
a storehouse of edibles.

The second one in line
has yet to take his turn;
he waits instead for hot
wheels and magical wings.

The youngest is enticed to go
before his trumpet blasts
to taste forbiddens before
his second teeth are out.

My hands are tightly
behind my back lest I reach
out and pull them back.

KAREN

I wait at a booth
for my daughter,
watch the young woman
with the open face, whose
hands I know so well.
I wait, after a quarter-century,
I waited, bonded to her
in a motherdaughter way.

She is my first born,
my only daughter.
My love for her runs deep
like ocean waters.

I recognize my genetic influence
in the slope of her shoulders,
the curve of her neck. I
recognize a style uniquely hers:
the tilt of her head, the curve
of her brow.

I learn from her the patience
of her pain, the freshness
of her smile.
We marched together
in sisterhood.
We sang in unison.

I beam love upon her,
born on the crest of a new age,
stoked by generations of
mothers and daughters,
improving with time.

GENETIC TRADITION

The curse is still with her, hanging around in the body
of a thirteen-year-old, son of the man who clomped
around the house draped in a blanket, throwing gloom
over life. She threw out the father only to watch
the veil of madness envelop the next in line.

When the son sits, legs crossed at an angle,
hands self-consciously playing about his face,
she sees before her the father. Through haze
of sleep she hears the younger male pace woodenfloors
where once his father walked, weeping tears
not dry from the generation before.

Should she speak slowly the myth of family agonies,
she would destroy the treachery masked behind a facade
of bonded loyalties   father to son   son to father.
Soft-cheeked where once a beard, one and the same,
they fear her turned back. The two belong together,
father grafted to son, clinging against a naked wall
light laying bare madness for all to see.

She does not fear their deaths, only ill-fated
patterns. Yet, father and son turn from each other, call
her name. The seed that grew within her womb, tainted
by pity, veiled in the name of love, sits before her.

They will not meet without her, will not acknowledge
their likenesses in each other's faces, turn to her
with words filled with venom, assured of her continued
presence, the stable commodity to which they alone own
rights. In the end, they long to merge and become one,
destroy each other with her as their witness.

NEAR GROWN

I see the fear in his eyes
the pain of not growing up right
sorrow of being afraid of the dark
though he stands tall like a man
his voice is deep like a leader
I see the doubt in his mouth
incompleteness of registering
for war having never left home
he longs to love a woman
I see ignorance in his chin
regret of not studying
of covering up gaps in information
though his language is slick
his boasting loud
I see the chaos large hands grabbing
onto the rope of order where buddies
dwell   he longs to join them

I hear him beg forgiveness
plead for recognition for he
was the first born son
whose deeds were marked
with false pride   I watch him
stand before me trembling
with anger   steady with the fear
the hope that I may abandon him
too soon before he is ready
to heal ropeburned palms   cut
ties securely knotted
I temper my anger   control
the urge to push him
from the playground into the world
where men carry guns
women supply the bullets

SON-FATHER RECONNECTING

It is Thanksgiving on the New Jersey Turnpike,
the heaviest traveled American road-day.
College-son sits beside his driver-father
after a three-month map-distance between them.
Two men together again in the divorced familial
bond made more poignant by the visiting quality
of a college son, juggling two homes, mother-father
rivalries, and two old habits of mother/son father/son
alliances, the dichotomy more harsh, more blatant
for manchild who only recently discovered his private
oneness away from the domestic clutter of parent-love,
stone and mortar and words—so many words—

lest he tighten the aching knot
between Fatherforce and him
between Motherforce and him
old young-eyes make the leaving possible,
but this sedate caterpillar son's four legs
balance indecisively, pieced together by their
separate parent needs, pieced together
in disobedience, so as not to remain
entombed

within their walls, like the chameleon
in his desert, he is free in unresponsive
silence and listens to the music,
part youth's impatience with the past
Father-son sit in small circled silence,
no longer valid for the scream the father
is holding in worries him because he cannot
hear it.

Being young grows harder every year.

The silent word on father and son lips is true,
the joy of love and despair of denial.
They expect much from each other.
It is enough for an honest beginning—
and the music—

WOMEN

A WOMAN'S REALITY

She spreads her table
with memories
first course served
in the dollhouse
hopscotch squares
dotted with chocolate kisses.
Main course a double entree
of couplets   marriage vows
joint bank accounts
with a side order of babies
pink and blue.
Dessert comes s l o w l y
after sips of love nectar.
A tart blue-penciled book
of life recipes as a woman.
The after-dinner drink
        is

        Solitude.

SHE ESCAPED

Cement brick blocks of time
uniform windows
regulation-size drapes
one table, three chairs,
one metal bed with nighttable,
squared-off cubicles
where old people dwell
asserting individuality
with the toss of a red tablecloth,
the throw of a needlepoint pillow,
the threadbare slipcover   from the south.

Institutionalized tenancy
at suppertime   shriveled grey-haired
menwomen sit by their windows sipping broth,
watching traffic.

As I drove to work one escaped;
stopped traffic on Washington Lane,
confused, walking the centerline in bathrobe
and muleslippers.
One morning as I drove to work an old
woman pressed her face against my windshield,
eyes wide, lips crooked. Cars weaved to avoid
hitting her; truckers blew foghorns. She
pointed skyward, her arthritic finger sharp
and white. Was she asking the way to heaven?
I left my car and approached her. Mistake off
she ran/walked, losing a muleslipper
in the middle of the road, her high-pitched groan
piercing the air.

They re-installed her behind cement brick blocks
of time to sit at the uniform window and peer
through the regulation-size drapes
of institutionalized tenancy.

ALICE'S HOUSE

Her home was snatched away,
all insulation gone. She stands there
bare and shivering, trying to communicate
with her sisters. Sisters underwent
the same basic training, she thinks.
But they turn away or secretly delight
in Alice's lost home, the one they have
always wanted.

Oh, single mother, attracted to Maurice,
snatching clandestine encounters
on staircases, coming and going.
She arouses him quietly before
children awaken, peers through cautiously
opened door for prying neighbors.
He slips out just after dawn.

Alice searching for a home in company
with the silent multitude, tears streaming
down her face, feels first stirrings
for a world out there where her only brother
waits in the Bay of Tonkin. Draftcards burn
while their owners chant, "one, two, three,
four, we won't go to war no more."
Alice has found a home.

She tries to fit too much into one life,
failing health, overwork for the revolution,
dishpan hands at the communal sink and overdue
papers for psychology one and contemporary social
problems. Her daughter is suspended from school
again. All along she tries to please others.

Golden Rick wants Alice to stay with him. He has
a curtained room. He writes there. She is drawn

to him. Political comrades, they are, carefully watched,
they sit around a wooden table, each at an assigned place
talking self-righteous rhetoric and quoting Mao.
Rick wants Alice to stay with him. But not for too long.

Alice searching for a home, pounding the cement, banging
on doors, looking in lighted windows into bare rooms
and empty eyes, encountering male obstacles as she tries
in vain to reach her sister. Alice returns her hands to the
       dishpan
and overworks for his hungry ego. Her
chores done, her timeclock punched, she takes up darning,
rocking back and forth on the broken rocker at Alice's
       house.

GARDENING

She was always
destroying things
that were important
to her
digging through
her garden
dirt lining her
fingernails and smudged
across her cheek
where she swatted a fly
resenting the fact
that weeds had lost respect.

MEETING UP WITH HER

Two years have passed since we last
met. She comes to volunteer her time
to help address envelopes for the
Norman Cousins Dinner. I feel
the difference.
I see the change.
I inquire.

Breast cancer, she replies,
a lumpectomy
chemotherapy
breast cancer, she replies,
her voice breathy, light
frequent giggles.

My own breasts ache suddenly.
I am full of questions.
I am full of her pain.
I am fearful for us women.

Breast cancer, she replies,
one day in; next day out;
they move fast;
breast cancer, she replies.

One in eleven, one in ten,
maybe one in six.
I count the number of women
in the room.
She is one; we are five.
Breast cancer, she replies.

FOR CHRISSA AT HER WEDDING

I remember decades ago when we met.
I remember setting your hair, dancing
around the sorority suite. I remember
blue books, shared boyfriends, midnight
hoagies. I remember discovery
that became knowledge
that became discovery. I remember.

I remember your first trip to California
where you sought solace, family patterns,
and your own truths. I remember your trip
to France, your linguistic ease with French,
with Russian. I remember your hopes
that became fear,
that became hope. I remember.

I remember the two of us wifing, birthing,
nursing our babies, early morning telephone
calls. I remember your first real job and
our weekly lunches. They were
personal, that became
professional, that
became personal. I remember.

I remember exploring existential questions,
as we formed an extended family. I
remember emergency calls, sleep-overs,
New York City doctor's visits and laughter
that became tears, that
became laughter. I remember.

I remember when our women's group began,
our feminism fullblown, our discontent,
our pride. We shared our deepest secrets,
recited our confessions, and dreams that
became realities, that became
dreams. I remember.

I remember the bond of single parenting,
five child-faces 'round a dining room table
on holidays and meaning that became
ritual that became meaning. I remember.

I remember theorizing about romance,
caution about love as you and Grant flew
East and West, evolving through your mutual
journey, guarding, yet recklessly risking
independence, that became dependence
that became interdependence.

Now two of you are one, building new memories on old
memories, which will become new dreams.

WOMANWRITER

This morning
I get up early
and begin to plant daisies
out behind the house.
Down on my knees
I remember to water
the seeds carefully.

When nighttime comes
I look for children
to put to sleep.
Stay, earth, long enough
for them to catch your song.

The future will look
at my work at the edge
of a threadbare field
going dark, where daisies
are painted yellow.

Women,
you know,
are painted
from the inside
where few men
have ever been.

UNSPOKEN COMMITMENT: A SESTINA

I.
Having lain with him
she remakes the bed
puts order in her
bedroom so long left
in disarray. She
lets the sunlight in.

II.
At night, she lies in
darkness, thoughts of him
rock her to sleep. She
moves about the bed
to the right, the left,
feeling him near her.

III.
He is far from her
for the moment, in
another place, left
to gather to him
what is dear. His bed
cold, it is not she

IV.
who lies nearby. She
has returned to her
cluttered room. Her bed
barren from with-in.
Dawn brings thoughts of him
she knows he has left.

V.
The warmth he has left
in her heart, this she
now recalls of him,
as he recalls her
still nestled with-in.
This now ordered bed

VI.
like a wedding bed
remembered once left
centuries with-in
when wifing. But she
is on fire with her
newborn sense of him.

VII.
A bed for love, she
left fear behind her
to rest within him.

THE SUBSTANCE OF OUR CONNECTION

Because I could not stop for Death,
He kindly stopped for me.

She was a woman who birthed two children,
a corner of her mind always alert to them.
She would not back into corners of compromise.
Her life kept its rewards as long as she gave
to others, through love, through friendship.

The carriage held but just ourselves

I see our heritage, a line of women
believing in tomorrow.

And Immortality.

One moment she was lace, a woman who
cherished dreams, self-reliant in her will.
Love unraveled like a tattered sweater,
leaving formless shreds which she gathered
and rewove into knitted beauty.

Italicized sections from "The Chariot" by Emily Dickinson.

AUSTRIAN FERN

When I take my work
to bed with me,
I surround the pillows
with plants
hide behind
the *Pinus ponderosa.*
In the morning
I will have to sever
the umbilical cord
and accept new authorities
at the office.

HER SON IS DEAD

i am afraid to rub against her open cut
a gash down the side of her face
that continues across her breasts.
my own stomach aches   contracts
expands   digested pain
a memory renewed for motherhood
for women who have birthed
and fed and weaned the young
now sent out to battle in wars
of which they know nothing.

i am gentle when she utters sounds
a moan   a groan   come forth
her lips   a thin line of unbearable
acceptance. my own are moist and
recite prayers to gods who spared me
this time 'round   my fate revealed
in another's grief for women
who tear loose aprons and
fill their sons' and daughters'
bellies with hot broth
for cold realities.

i am calm before a stony
path of unknown tragedies
hidden in chance
in case we women get too
smug about birth. my sons
are taller than the crown of my
head   towering infernos who rush
into burning buildings   heroic
deeds in the name of martyr.

i am cold when my bereaved friend
shivers   hot when labor overcomes her
she survives — though barely —what
would have felled me. i am putting
cream on her scars   helping them heal
lessening the drawing up of taut
new skin regenerated in sleep.

AND NOW THEY CALL HER DOCTOR

Adult she was
un-degreed with diaper pail
and bottles, housework repeated.
Half-years of college campuses,
graduation ceremonies denied
delayed detoured:

A Bachelor of Arts

Chained to bedposts wifing,
mothering

A Master's Degree

the following year. Male nomenclatures,
misfitting the mistress of the house.

Now they call her Doctor,
dissertation typed at night
when family slept. Now they call her doctor,
so long she healed others.

Doctor of Philosophy

healing love of learning, male degrees
set aside by a woman whom now
they call doctor.

VIEW FROM TWIN PEAKS, SAN FRANCISCO

I browse secondhand clothing stores,
in Haight-Ashbury,
where I think I will find
recycled hippie-shirts I wore during sit-ins.

I walk by Alice Walker's house,
back and forth, hoping she will
come out to play.
We ride the cablecar in Chinatown,
hang on the rail, up steep hills,
down car chase bumps.

I stand above the city,
fog obscuring the base
of the golden bridge,
listen to foreign tongues
at lookout points
overseeing rooftops.

I hear voices on San Francisco
streets, sounds from twenty years
ago, protest sounds, student
demonstrations, beatnik rhythms
still hang in the air
above Twin Peaks.

FUTURE WORRIES

The other side of me
is a bag lady, who wears
all she owns, grubs for food
in overturned trash cans, while
I make monthly mortgage payments,
keep up my old house so I won't
be turned out on the street.

The other side of me
is a bindlestiff, who picks
up fragmented information
out in the cold, sleeps
on the pavement by a heating
vent. I go to work daily,
always on time, reliable employee,
so I will have good references
should I need them.

I may look upstanding
but my existence is tenuous,
teeters between upward mobility
and insecure hoarding of frozen
dinners for consumption
because

the other side of me
is a bag lady, who wanders lost,
homeless on streets
with too many corners.

COUPLING

'TWAS ALMOST A HOUSE BY THE SEA

Debussy plays in rhythm to the breathing of a dog
wet from dives in and out of the river, sandy
from skipping in beachheads. Papers scatter
in winds warmed by salty air.
Violins build
arabesques
remind the man of a woman young,
the woman of the man in youth
running across meadows.
The man calls out in sleep,
"Bring the boys home! Bring
the boys home!" away from national
guardsmen who killed tomorrow
at Kent State.

The woman hesitates,
steps back, recalls snow
drifts near another life
when they met clandestinely
behind columns. The woman
smiles privately, steps lightly over pages torn
from the bible. The man's chest
heaves, inhales new ideas,
exhales angry recall.

The woman catches her reflection
flicks back graying hair
once black like nights in the Algarve.
The man's hand falls upon the dog,
soothes canine instinct.
The woman remembers his stroke,
when words would not come, a voice now sings;
when muscles were paralyzed, now move legs
down country roads.
The man
The woman
The dog
The moonlit doorway.

LIVING TOGETHER

some days it is as if we are an old married couple
in the habit of loving offhandedly   sleeping
side by side like two old calicoes raised from the same
litter   we kick sand in each other's faces
some nights it is as if we are victims
of housing shortages   fighting inflation   pooling
moneys   like two old brothers on welfare

some afternoons I ponder residency taken
for granted   signed in stupor after random
nights of thrashing about on sheets
writing dreams of faceless men who seduce

some mornings I awaken surprised   bathroom
occupied   we are roommates   long graduated
having passed exams with no bearing on the future

some mornings prepared coffee greets me
a state of mind   falling into rhythm without dissent

some nights I long to confront nuances
the habit growing into comfort   some nights
I fall asleep in your arms   rarely forgetting poetic
license   hoping you will call later from a
telephone booth   send anonymous flowers

some full moons I stand at the window while
you sleep   watching bindlestiffs sleeping
in doorways   stray cats   familial felines
homelessly whoring.

OASIS

When it rains I water the plants,
carefully considering how it would be
for them out of captivity.

I rotate the potted foliage
give the *Gloxinia* a chance
to receive sunlight first.
The African violet droops
I surround it with Wandering Jews.

I am careful not to drown the roots
of the Tiger plant by overwatering.
They need drainage. I pull off
dead leaves at random.

You watch me talk to the plants.
A smile slowly spreads across your
mouth, your eyes, your brow. I
gently touch the fern before stroking
your arm. I spray a mist of water
on the leaves and moisten
your lips with my tongue.

PLUPERFECT

Different pasts, different presents, different futures
He, first born male; I, last female
Different patterns, parenting rooted in Dorsey;
I, in Presley; twenty-five when I was birthed.

He sleeps the day; I, the night, drawing children near
whom he repels, rejecting acid rock, respecting
traditional degrees. No more perseverance for what
I have begun to respect; buried beneath sour sense
of humor while I laugh.
The artist opposing the politician.
Sexual drives change lanes on opposite sides of streets.

Integrity will rot as I watch the differences.
I will sneak about, grabbing young limbs, recreational
fun shot to hell by speech patterns, memories
of generational differences.

Different pasts, same presents, same futures.
He, love child, moonchild as I; waits for me
to come of age.

He sleeps beside me as we draw offspring of various
ages around us. No difference. His are mine; mine his.
Rejecting property divisions, together the scenery is lush.
The artist complementing the politician who lends
perspective to moody swings. Sexual maple syrup,
smooth as molasses.

Integrity stronger for the sharing, for the spanned
intelligence, understanding all ages with no secrets.
No deceit possible. Twenty-five years are mere minutes
ticking away on the clock beside our bed.

SEASONING

He loves me without license
crime his incentive
shoplifting for excitement
I wish the weather would change
and we were making love again
if my heart were stronger
he would be twenty years younger
his arms taut with pulling muscles
legs slightly bowed
from the weight
of my body pressed into his

once I juggled four lovers
held them at a distance
now his proximity is sharp
yes, it is love I feel
I am not depending on false gods
to seal this lover's fate
I would rather be wife
than legally not belong
I remember when I wifed
I seem not to forget those
nagging responsibilities

yet I have all the tasks
none of the rewards
if I were his wife I would be
protected on the outside
vulnerable on the inside,
where pain is more acute

and when the weather changes
sun will warm my courage

LOVE POEM

She dreamed of meeting a man of forty,
worldly, older but young enough; someone
whose temples had begun to gray, whose
eyes revealed wisdom.
She will not have as much time with him
as she would have had with the Greek sailor,
the Roman drummer. She was five when he
was thirty. Her first was a day younger
the second ten years younger   then two years
older then five years older   then he fooled
her with slick muscles and young tender hands.
They eat persimmons in the garden. He makes
love like a boy of eighteen, a man of fifty;
combining tenderness with experience.
She will not have as much time with him.
She is sad for that.
She is glad for him.

His eyes speak more eloquently than words,
his look, his voice soft pliant, ready
to search secrets of her body.
It is as though their hearts have found
knowledge beyond their lives,
black hair mingled with silver
making him more hers, a touch
easier to love than perfection
would have been. He is her family
barely born   having nothing to do
with distance from things that
separate them. Close to her,
fragile love — he is her home in life;
he is her life in death.

ON A VERMONT PORCH

Jack and Rose live up in Vermont.

Each has a wooden rocker, a pine table
             between them.

First of every month they switch
             places.

Rose is rock outside, soft putty
             inside.

Jack built the house hard
             like iron.

They change places, alternate watchtower
             poses.

Jack remembers to watch the
             calendar.

Time to change places, her books
             resituated.

His reading glasses move to the other
             side.

Last month, Jack's view was
             mountains.

This month he contemplates
             Harvey's Lake.

Rose has a turn at the full sun
             rays.

They smile. They are
             silent.

No mention of time marked by repositioned
             rocking chairs.

Jack and Rose live up in Vermont.

DUST TO DUST

We sit under the gazebo
on the banks of Tom's River.
You want to discuss where I
will throw your ashes.
I change the subject.
We recall the winter the river
froze; cars rode across.
It is a clear day.
We can see across to the
other side where Seaside Heights
houses rest at water's edge.

It is a lonesome relationship,
this decade-old alliance that
defies statistics where we two
go beyond ourselves, beyond
children whom we birthed,
but only I, the mother, felt life
come from my womb.
We speak of your grandson who
fished two years ago at this spot
with his grandfather. You persist,
"Stand on the pier and toss
the ashes out to the water."
Again I change the subject.

I will deal with the ashes when
I have to deal with the ashes.

GOLDENBIRD

He is filled with warmth
and sensitivity as we walk
in the rain, remembering our
plans for Bastille Day in Paris.
Geminis should sit together,
he suggests, he in his car,
I, in mine.

In my house we do not touch
over children's heads. One
makes him coffee; another
kisses his cheek. I stand
aside and watch them touch
him in places where I have been.

I cover them with embraces
and look love at him without
touching. When they return
from him I feel his presence
in their skin and weep.

Yeats' Golden Bird was content to sing of what is past, or passing,
or to come.

MARRIAGE

   I remember early days,
we were new to Chicago,
unused to living together.
I remember your eyes small
in sleep, large in anger.
I remember the sound
of traffic outside your bedroom
window. I remember the night
you did not come home. I
remember labor pains coming
in waves, tightening promises
we whispered once. I remember
your clenched fists beating
on the wall, punching holes
through my illusions. I remember
the feel of your arms around me,
begging me to stop what I was
powerless to change. I remember
deceptive phrases, clues to the other
side of a faithless husband. I
remember surprise at not feeling
guilt after the first time.

   I remember childfaces
around the diningroom table listening
to blasphemous parents tear
apart earth from under their feet.
I remember wanting to say, "Stop!"
There had to be a mistake. This man,
this woman were different. I
remember the taste of blood when
my teeth bore down on my lower lip,
choking words of forgiveness.
I remember the last time we made love.
You took it as a sign of reconciliation.

I gave it as a wife's last obligation.
I remember washing away seeds
of discontent, hot words that froze
our emotions in midair.

    I remember how I pictured what time
would bring, the two of us alone,
the children gone from home. I
remember closing my eyes, trying
to lighten your hair with gray, thin
it with time. I remember feeding you
well to pad you from illness. It took more
strength than I had, more faith in men.
I remember.   I remember.

I DO NOT FORGIVE YOU

When I took your name I weeped
for an unrequited bloodline.
You covered me with paychecks,
doled out allowance to cover
wifely chores. Children brought
your slippers while I washed dishes,
the newspaper awaited your attention;
later I read your underlinings, gleaning
high points of larger questions.

Smells waked me at night,
remembrance of college degrees left
to rot in a closet. Apartment filled
with clutter on Sundays. Monday
the emptiness of married promises made
in the dark, too young to understand
obedience. Remnants of passionate
beginnings held onto me, even when I
saw deception in your eyes; I held on,
sure of suffocation, afraid
of starvation.

We paid the lawyers well,
went our separate ways. We
are tied by knots of birth,
of shared children, dead pets.
My name remains your name,
under pretense of clannish
loyalties; yet, I am nameless
from lost generations.

My name is nobody,
a family name wrought
with allegiances
to faceless representatives
of tradition.

TELEVISIONPHONES

They are coming out with these new
television telephones,
the ones that send a video
along with the voice
so that two callers can see
each other as they talk.
We have communicated by
telephone for forty years,
first as young playmates,
then as teenage steadies.
In college it was our link
to the past.
After thirteen years we
reconnected as parents
married to strangers.

Now and then we miss a year
or two. When we have been
together we are well prepared
and staged. An affair,
a friendship, reunions that
saw us through births
and deaths and divorce,
birthday wishes, gossip,
counsel and solace.

Now they are coming out
with video-telephones.
I will block the screen.

THE COUPLE

The signs were there
erratic responses
bland confusion

He accompanies her to the
beauty parlor twice a week,
his index finger at her chin,
he balances her precarious
wits to focus her still
large eyes on his
a reality check.

Her white hair is coiffed
to restore the beauty he
still sees when he looks at her.

She is in another world,
coming out in spurts to tease
him. "Look at my new bracelet,"
she says. "My husband gave it to me."
A medical bangle, solid gold love
inscribed with her disease
lest she wander off.

BESIDES, SHE SAID

Nevertheless he is immature.
I wanted a man of fifty, rounded
with experience, over the hump of male
malice that hits about the same time
as middle-aged spread.

Talked out of loving before the oven
is warm enough to heat hot biscuits
of emotion, before it is too late to
turn back, cancel the order for
friendship and bedding and planning
those lovers' intrigues
that so elude me.

But potential that is poignant presumes
early abortion of any chance of committing
to more than dinner at a fast food
spot on the freeway.

Besides he is not in the Arts. No
beard, no literary references, not even
acrylic paint on his elbows nor clay
on his scuffed oxfords, so bourgeois
yet frumpy like a drop-out
gone corporate.

'Tis facile to stop this madness before
emotions hook into emotions, yet I
suspect that his emotions are counterfeit,
copies of early movies seen in
the sixties as protest programs.

Besides, he is not my type.
Yet, I feel as though I missed
riding the crest of a wave
amid saline azure calm.

A PLAY OF TIME

He has a plan in mind,
interludes of scheduled love.
Heated emotions harden under quick
cooled separations. I resist
melting and freezing new passion,
afraid layers thickened like volcanic
lava camouflage joy.

Yet, I feel his knowing of me.
I trust his orchestration, maestro
of Bartok concertos whose baton
points out flaws and perfections.

I suspect he is playing with me.
His humanness rolls around my mind,
erects barriers, excuses to cancel.
Reason damns emotions, orders me
back to my senses.

Of time,
          I have plenty
                    enough
for him to take up horseback riding,
                    enough
so that he can stabilize his
                    eccentricities
that drew me to him at the start

Yet, I trust his knowledge, his desire
to stop me from mucking up, his strong back
rushing open closed doors of silence
that call to me to flee in time
to justify an ancient script,
                    a palimpsest
carved on walls of Neanderthal caves.

BESIDE YOU AND THE SEA

The incessant pounding of the surf
reaches down into my soul, where
sorrow dwells in a loveless chasm.
I awaken beside you, and watch you
in sleep, a place that softens you.

Last night I glimpsed the other side
of your loving: hard places, undeveloped
corners clipped short as the jetty
outside our bedroom window breaks
the flow of the sea.

I close my eyes to block your echoing
words of denial, a shield wrapped around
your dreams. I reach inside, scoop up
raw emotions, soft and new.

I recite our flaws over and over to myself,
reminders of how tenuous love is.
The ocean water is patient, persistent,
rolling back the sand, spilling saltwater
tears. The primitive rhythm beats me
a warning:

> Come Away
> Drift Away
> Float Away

back where we two were launched.

Truth is whispered in the incessant
pounding of the surf, washed away
with tides that leave hard shells
in their wake.

CROSSING

We flirted with attraction,   innuendoes
woven among confessed secrets. His eyes
laughed my jokes, winked encouragement.

> Last night I saw his closed eyes
> absorb pleasure from our touch
> his mouth on my breast, his legs
> around mine. His hands guided mine
> as we lay in the dark, dizzy
> without sleep, resistance low.

I do not know what emotion I feel for this friend,
so unlike past lovers. He is on the brink of my soul,
somewhere beyond the periphery of truth, poised
on ambivalence. I somersault back to the other side
where touch is a mere amenity between friends.

> Last night I slept in his arms,
> our skin familiar with pleasure.
> His voice took me into the realm
> of possibility where man and woman
> join like the base of a thick oak.

I strain to recapture impersonal intimacy.
I erase images of holding him inside me,
blink away memories of pulsating passion
and mounting pleasure.

> Last night I tasted juices
> of his manhood as I lay open as a
> fallen acorn, my shell cracked.

He does not recognize my desire for taking him
inside, cleaving him to me in that woman-man way.
In daylight, we resume our rightful positions,
while I mask raw emotions.

Last night the seeds were sown
for a rich forest in which we will lose
ourselves to undergrowth
and green foliage of love.

MARRIAGE PLANS

I sit in this small room,
without ventilation, without
permanence, and pound broken
typewriter keys, hoping you will
surprise me, bring me a proper
machine, crisp ironed curtains.
I stop such daydreams; they are too
familiar, trying to make over my
lover to reinforce my sense
of independence.

We two were friends; yet there is a slow
pain rising in my chest, warning
of impending danger. This I keep
in check, despite my inability to
swallow food lumpier than tepid soup.
Sometimes the knot drops, and my bowels
twist until your arms are around me, which
is why we hang on, I at your house,
you at mine; as if we know nights together
prevent turning from this commitment.

The best surprises keep me loving
you while disappointments keep
me loving myself.

AQUA

You were sure it was a case
of early menopause; I was
confident it was premarital jitters;
    but
the test tube showed aqua.
The fact was there before us:
conception.

The night I miscarried followed
a day of fatigue, a sense
of foreboding. Cramps were well
    spaced,   bleeding
clotted and erratic.

I keep the aqua evidence in my
bureau drawer, a reminder.
A baby appears in my dreams.
Sleep reveals a deep mourning,
a hollow pit scooped from my womb.

We do not speak of loss.
My reproductive organs wait a
respectable period of time to
resume their menstrual cycle,
now rescheduled to disrupt
our wedding day.

My bleeding womb is witness
to the silence.

SECOND MARRIAGE

Sometimes I hear
the first wife
inside of me
call out sharp barbs.
She does not yet know
her place in my new life,
does not understand, has
not caught up with me.

Sometimes in my dreams
I am but twenty, and he
is an image counterimposed
on the face of my first husband.

Sometimes I forget that I have
known others.

HE IS MY HUSBAND

I see him walk across the street
unaware that I am watching.
I hear him on the telephone,
his voice familiar, intimate.
I taste his salty skin
with my morning coffee.

Perchance his name comes up
at a meeting, his photograph
appears in the morning paper,
his handwriting on a check.

I circle back to get
a second look, a reminder.

If I close my eyes I recall
our first meeting,
the way he suddenly appeared
in my dreams.

A ROSE

We weathered changing seasons, the four moon phases
that altered our external world—snow-covered river,
sand beach summer, autumn equinox of flaming
red trees — marked in the beginning by the last
rose of summer in Cape Cod as we honeymooned.

The sweet rose smell of intimacy on brassbed sheets
marks our private time, hours when thorns
of resistance are clipped, and the soft petal
of commitment caresses our souls.

The pace erratic, seesawing our emotions, hour-
to-hour, only to settle into this loving bond
surrounding the sum of such moments,
wrapping us tightly into a year of spiritual
depth, cocooning us in tall willowy trees,
in low growing rose bushes.

At one year's end we face the richness
of such loving—the survivor symbol
marking our first anniversary,

   whose petals will fall,
   enrich the soil,
   deepen the roots,
   nourish the earth.

WITH TIME

You, my husband, were patient as I thrashed
into wifing. Tonight I feel the wife-role
knowledge emerging from our
honeymooned chaos.

Today, I said, "You feel like family."
It is as if we grew up together, though
this union is not a year old. Six months ago
we struggled through awkward silences,
groped for strings to tighten our
connection. Tonight I understand your sense
of justice, the way you walk city streets,
drive the outskirts above posted speed limits.

We are siblings out in public, a knowing
glance confirms our private thoughts.
We are parents at home, fresh smelling
laundry piled on a table. We are lovers,
too, cutting through everyday tasks
with the sharp blade of passion.

Tonight, lying beside you, in the dark,
bone-to-bone, in the black night, I
dive in and out of sleep. The wind
blows cold outside our window.

I am warmed by your flesh.
I am quieted by your skin,
by your gentle touching
of my protected corners.

Tonight, we pierce the veils
of marriage and glimpse the
serenity of family.

SUMMER BEACH

The sand beach smells
damp towels from the constant
Atlantic are familiar like gritty
beach shirts, damp for months.
I lose David to his private dreams
that crest with the waves
and crash to reality.

I am stirred by visions, memory
playback against my closed lids,
film stills shown out of sequence...

> wave swallowing me
> caught in undertow
> Spanish dunes
> my children bent on haunches
> as they fill pails and build
> sand castles, their father
> trying to be subtle as
> he eyes passersby.

Beside me in midlife drifts my
second husband, respectfully silent
to camouflage tempered truths.

In past lives, men lay with me
on the beach, brought me shells
and sea gifts. There are no such gifts
with David—but contemplation.

I stop my hand from taking his as he
succumbs to mental acrobatics
cartwheeling petty complaints
into something I cannot touch.
I rub sunscreen on his still white
limbs, imitating primal worlds where
animals consort with the sea.

Virginia Woolf put stones in her
pockets and walked into the water.

LOST HUSBAND

We are no longer
man and wife
we are nothing
we never were
woman and husband
only man and wife once
we are nothing
now—no relation
no blood
no friendship
when I see you
I cannot focus
clearly I cannot
remember
having lain with you
we are nothing
we cannot touch
or speak or cry
and once
we were man
and wife.

OF DEFENSES

My love for him began
as the snow
falling on our front lawn
this silent night.
I needed a clear path
to escape the madness
of habitual dominance.
I shoveled my way clear,
an embankment rising on
either side, as the shovel
of seclusion dug out the ice
and tossed it into a pile.
He calls my distractions
indifference, and my wifing
chores possessive gestures.

It is about survival
and self-love. It is a common coupling,
that has reduced me to this state of self-
absorption, for tightly
wound commands chopped up
my once soft affections
and the pieces have reassembled.

He mistakes my self-
defense for hardness.
I used to draw warmth from fire
until flames burned my skin.

THROUGH A LOOKING GLASS

A man
A woman
A mirror
reflects soft spots
and steel-lined
chips of pain.

His face glows from the fire
of fear in his belly.
Her face twists with efforts
to mask her push for self-control.

A woman is measured by things
she cannot control.
She is measured by where she is
flat or round.
Let her be measured,
if a woman is to be measured,
by the things she controls,
by who she is trying to become.

Her face dulls from disappointment
in her heart.
His face sobers as he tests
his own strength.

A man is measured by things
he can control.
He is measured by what he says
by what he does.
Let him be measured,
if a man is to be measured,
by the things he cannot control,
by where he has been and who
he is trying to become.

A woman
A man
A crack in the looking glass.

COCKTAILS TO GO

NEWS ITEMS

Phillip Worthington
will remember in years to come
the week he made national news
stolen from Grandview Hospital
by Ramona Thompson, a stranger hungry
for a baby to fill her barren womb.
She took him to Sellersville Holiday Inn.
She took him as her own.

He remembers familiar arms of the woman
who birthed him, lips moist against his skin,
breasts full.

He will remember as in a dream
roughly dreamt.

Tanya,
I try to envision the madness, the urgency
that twisted your maternal extincts, that
turned your hands into weapons, that pushed
your infant son under the bathwater.

I hear the air bubbles gurgling up in the
tub, teasing you, tempting you. I envision
you later, standing at the kitchen sink,
trying to chop the infant body
into manageable pieces.

This joint up here, like a chicken wing,
cut at the gristle, hipbone displaced,
neck hard to penetrate. A small torso
wrapped in newspaper, tossed into a creek.

I know you were insane, Tanya. I suspect
you want to reverse time, go back
to the bathroom, pull out the stopper
in the tub, drain insanity. Instead
the scene escalated, the film kept going,
the plot, like your baby's blood, clogging
up the drain, thickened.

I know you were insane, Tanya.

WASHINGTON SQUARE

women-hands push swings
                    back and forth
                    back and forth

rock the baby
walk the aardvark
tease pigeons
brush flies
                    back and forth
                    womeneyes

guard chastity
plug tears
do not surrender
to aching arches
bound upright
                    back and forth
                    back and forth

labor hands itch
to open unread books
left on benches for idle
moments that do not come

she has not come
in three months
rocking on the bed
                    back and forth
                    back and forth

ODE TO WALTER MACKEN

I fancy a leprechaun read my palm
outside Liberty Hall where comrades
rise in silence for Bernadette's recovery.
Seven bullets by three would-be assassins,
her three children witnesses. Later we drive to Portalois,
    fortress where roof
binoculars burn my back. I puff
a cigarette, and glare at Britlovers.

Condemned comrade sentenced to hang.
    "They'll not get my fuckin' head,"
    he says, hands shaking.
Death by hanging, common prison burial
beside Kevin Barry
    Aye
Ireland summons her children to the flag,
to the brotherhood. Remember me in vaults
of St. Michans. Bernadette lies healing
in Belfast. I sip Bewley's coffee,
keep patient counsel, the birth of death
dull pounding passing through.
    Aye
River Liffey was our witness.
Mrs. O'Neill died last August.

DEATHING

Voices of the dead call out to newly inducted
soldiers, "Come in, come in! Rape and reap
your spoils in the name of Freedom, in the name
of christoursavior, of jesusourlord, in the name
of yahweh, come in, come in, martyr us for history
books, mark us for slaughter!"

See the bones piled on an open field,
limbs this way, that, twisted out of shape
like symmetry of convenience, hollow eyes
gape unconscious, a mother's hand frozen
around her child's small fingers. Smell
rotten fires, stench of mottled minds,
constructed gas chambers reserved for fringed
shawls, old bearded rabbis whose eyes froze
heavenward in spellbound nirvana
forsaken by the godofmoses.

Arms tattooed, numbers remind nuclear physicists
of atomic activity tested at hiroshima in the name
of peace, burned pieces of soul spanned
continents of germanytojapan human scapegoats
feast on tin cans as mountain goats bleat
in hills above a PLO camp or in manzanar.

See the children in an open field,
hungry stomachs distended, swollen fingers
hollow eye sockets. See them stand around,
beg for food, for a touch, a puncture so
that blood will prove their veins flow:
proof of existence, of having
witnessed such madness.

OBIT

He was always rejecting
people
who were important
to him,
slamming doors
in faces
when friends
got too familiar,
falling asleep
when his wife
got into his bed,
resenting
mortality.

BULKHEAD TO DEMOCRACY

The bulkhead stands, weathered by time,
persistent, a wooden wharf separates public
from private beaches. Crevices are worn
enough to admit wash from boat wakes.
It is a token gesture.

When the river is quiet, traffic lanes clear,
the bulkhead reigns as a solid reminder
of things that tear asunder, that keep
inequality constant as the classes know
their places, so residents do not overstep
territories. They accept boundaries.

When there is plenty, water is turbulent.
Waves crest high, break against the generous
bulkhead. It is a symbolic sacrifice,
river water contaminated by debris ridden
brackish elements form the other side.
It is a gesture to keep fires of hope burning.
Just enough to inspire the next generation.

NUCLEAR WINTER

It is different this winter
Sounds of children's laughter silent
people gone to another place another time
leaving the job of canning to monkeys who
do as they saw done in the old order

The winterfrost coats their tongues
with white heat   salivating canines
desire carnivorous repasts   rare blooded
people whose turn it is to wait
for the food dish to be placed
before them   lapped up on command

The winterwind howls in the night
cries out to the young   to the old who
walk patiently to breadlines   hands
outstretched   mouths dry with fever
as the untamed spoon portions
to hold them until new sunsets

The winterrain is cold   pierces weary
bones   resigned to wait for a turnover
in old guard   recycling priorities   legal
tender now matches and batteries
and precious metals to measure riches

the wintersnow falls silently
on blanched bones   attracting
dogs who howl at midnight   run
in packs   pawprints clear
on newly whitened fields

The wintermoon carries sounds
of howling wolves who wander fields
happen upon cement sidewalks
search for a change in survival
The fit become the unfit   the unfit
fixtures of leadership

VERMONT A DECADE LATER

Young mother, I was, escaped wife
lost in wooded contemplation
chanting endlessly, weeping clear
mountain water for lost womanhood,
forgotten promises. Faces of sisters
bound to the soil surrounded my fear,
listened to my self-indulgent cries.
Farm men plowing truth into crops,
sweat cleansing me of city smut,
offered strong muscle to lift me high
above banal loyalties. They sent me
back unwillingly, through drifted snow,
beyond green mountains, above the flow
of syrupped maples.

I made the pilgrimage but three times
from diapered babes and barely
weaned husbandry to a community of artists
plotting next year's revolution.

I return a woman unshackled,
nameless now as generations of sisters
invent pseudonyms. Wooded hollows
newly overgrown with twisted vines
calling greetings to an old friend.
I meet up with my past, grasping for new
scapegoats, sleeping in an open field
of emotion, dreaming I am home again,
a refugee adrift. I bring sacrifices
to easily forgotten altars, my head bent
in humble reverence. I walk over paths
trailblazed in angry rebellion, the heat now
cool, trees bending to the wind as I bend
to drink from mountain tarns

my eyes meet my reflected self, the one
middleaged, the other ripe
with maidenhood, the truth
whispered between them.

TOWARD SUNLIGHT ALONE

the rose is obsolete
        —William Carlos Williams

Spring is hospitable
the old courtesy
of life for life.

I stop for a moment,
beckoned into the forest
to wrestle with a young sapling.

Last year's roots
re-germinate and prosper
in a superb phantasmagoria
of off-colored blossoms.

I press my forehead
to an unyielding
tree trunk, a hardness
to hold onto, for all time
breaking the silence of the woods.

The sky is an endless stretch,
threaded with cotton, smudged by a passing plane.

Nothing so simple
as a single perfect cloud
but an infinitude
persistently pausing overhead.

TRANSFORMATION

Last night I lost track of time.
As I turned out the house lights,
a barren field outside reflected
off the moonlight.

Today I awaken to a sudden
burst into prominence
of candelabra-like stalks
pushing into the sky.

Several large pines bend
to the wind as they adjust
to their new habitat.
Smaller spruce trees
imitate the land slope and
present a united frontal view
from my bedroom window.

Our neighbors planted trees
at strategic points
of separation
along our property lines.
The landscape is transformed
by three truck-loads of plantings,
carefully placed along the hemline
of the surveyor's skirted markings.

I am thankful for their
green grace, for their
full figured night shadows,
for their sun-screening breadth
when the afternoon sun is high,
for the pose they strike,
for the tenure freely granted.

I watch the landscape for signs
that might tell me something more
of the something less I sense inside.

ACKNOWLEDGMENTS

"A Woman's Reality" was the recipient of the NY National Poetry
   Anthology Prize, 1986, and of the Amherst Society Dickinson
   Award, 1992.
"Gardening" was published in the University of Pennsylvania literary
   magazine *A Voyage Out*, 1976, and in *International Poetry Review*,
   1983.
"Womanwriter" was published in *Tuesday Nights Magazine*, 1976.
"Austrian Fern" was published in *International Poetry Review*, 1983.
"Future Worries" was published in *World Poetry*, 1984, and in *Voices Israel*,
   vol. XXI (1993).
"Kiev" was the recipient of the Northeastern States Poetry Contest,
   Honorable Mention, 1986, and of the Amherst Society Dickinson
   Award, 1988; it was published in *Voices Israel*, vol. XX.
"In the Synagogue" was published in *Israel Horizons*, vol. XXXIX, no. 3 of
   4 (Sept./Oct. 1991).
"A Test of Faith" was published in *Best Poems by 297 Eminent Poets in 77
   Countries*, World Poetry, India, 1992.
"When the Children Are Grown" was published in *Muse's Brew Poetry
   Review*, 1984.
"Building Bridges" was published in *Perceptions*, Fall 1991.
"Twas Almost a House by the Sea" was published in *Expressions, First
   State Journal*, vol. II, no. 1 (Spring/Summer 1987); *The Poetry
   Center*, 1988; Honorable Mention, *Poetry Center Anthology*, 1989;
   Voices Israel, vol. XIX; Rueben Rose winner, 1991.
"Living Together" was published in *The International Poetry Review*, vol.
   IX (1983); *Voices Israel*, vol. XIX (1991); *CPU Review*, vol. I, no.
   2 (Oct. 1991), second prize; JD Johnson Memorial Award-
   Honorable Mention, *Poet Magazine*, 1993.
"Oasis" was published in *Bitterroot Magazine*, 1978.
"Seasoning" was published in *Dan River Anthology*, 1987.
"Dust to Dust" was published in *Z Miscellaneous*, vol. II, no. 1 (Jan. 1988).
"Crossing" was published in *Poetry Center*, 1988; Triton College Contest
   winner, 1989; *Ariel*, vol. VIII (1989).
"Aqua" was published in *Z Miscellaneous*, vol. II, no. 1 (Jan. 1988).
"Bulkhead to Democracy" was published in *Best New Poets of 1987*.
"Vermont a Decade Later" was published in *The American Poetry
   Anthology*, 1983.
"Through a Looking Glass" was published in *World Poetry Society*, 1992.
"Obit" was published in *The International Poetry Review*, 1983.
"Lost Husband" was published in *Poetry Center*, 1987.
"Substance of Our Connection" was published in *The International
   Anthology, Many Voices, Many Lands*, vol. II, no. 1 (1988).
"Mentalhospital" was published in *The International Poetry Review*, 1989.
"Toward Sunlight Alone" was published in *Poet Magazine*, vol. IV, no. 3
   (Winter 1992/93); recipient of the I.M. Williams Award.
"As a Mother" was published in *Moods and Mysteries*, vol. IV, Poetry
   Press.